Valentine's Day in the Mummy Museum

poems by

David Allan Cates

Finishing Line Press
Georgetown, Kentucky

Valentine's Day in the Mummy Museum

ACKNOWLEDGMENTS

"Why I Don't Need Adrenaline-Rush Recreational Activities" and "Luna"
were published in *Willow Springs.*
"Regret" and "Whatever Happened to Them" in the *American Journal of
Poetry.*
"Aid" is forthcoming in a Scablands Press anthology, *Evergreen.*
"Valentine's Day in the Mummy Museum" and "People Are Saying" in
Sheila-Na-Gig online.
"And My Country Loved Me" and "Blue" and "Good Luck" in the *High
Desert Journal.*
"Not Quite Fall" in *Verse Virtual.*
"For a Boy I Knew" in *The Talking River Review.*
"On A Cliff With You" in *The Sun* magazine.
"The Newlyweds Next Door," in *Poems Across the Big Sky II*, an anthology.
"What With Light We Might Imagine" in *MexicoCityLit.*
"Now What," "San Pedro Sula," "Maybe This Time," "Waiting for Breakfast,"
"What I Want," "Solitude," "Young French Lovers," "The Mysterious Location
of Kyrgyzstan," "You Could Have Had Me," "Morning People," "The Purpose
of Kissing," "For the Uncountable Time," and "You and Me and the Dead"
first appeared in the chapbook, *THE MYSTERIOUS LOCATION OF
KYRGYZSTAN*, Satellite Press, 2016

Publisher: Leah Huete de Maines
Editor: Christen Kincaid
Cover Art: R. David Wilson, painting *Una noche con milagros*
Author Photo: Leland Buck
Cover Design: Elizabeth Maines McCleavy

Order online: www.finishinglinepress.com
       also available on amazon.com

Author inquiries and mail orders:
Finishing Line Press
P. O. Box 1626
Georgetown, Kentucky 40324
U. S. A.

Table of Contents

Baskets of Purple Garlic

for Mike and Donna

Our House

In the kitchen masked residents count apples
and sort beans, pound yams or slap *masa* into tortillas.
Everybody's taking pictures and sending them
to each other. Of course, we'd been warned it all ends
eventually, but like the irritating memory
of a dear friend gone mad and missing, or of a car
swerving wacky at the wrong time to take a brother,
death was a downer. I mean, we'd thought about it
discreetly, on tip toe, and mostly ascribed it
to character flaws. But now—*duh*—it's like we're all
on acid at the same time and really *getting* it,
I mean, *feeling* it, which explains the glazed eyes
around the table after we eat. We're not exactly sure
how it started, but that night when Theo cranked
the opera to ten and the soprano's voice burrowed
under our skin, we all *knew* we *knew* a butterfly
had opened its wings and through the window
wind shook the treetops and scattered the stars.
McDougal said, *Is this the only tea you have?* and Riker
said, *It's never been anything different*, by which
nobody had a clue what he meant except everything
was suddenly very beautiful. I was looking
for my socks in the shadow in the corner on my knees
when Kiki first began to cry. No escape,
we stood in a circle holding hands. It was clear
we didn't all believe whatever we'd once believed—
private things, like our own groovy destiny,
or how the gadget we'd been making in the garage
would change the world—*ha!* Or public things,
like how our people rose from the bog, or dollars
are better than pesos. To cheer up we put our right foot in,
and our right foot out. Then our right foot in again,
which was fun until Natasha accused Chen of cheating
and the guns came out of hiding. *Talk*, Nico said,
but most of us stared dumbly at our feet, mine still
without socks. Bridger said, *This is like living
dog years*, and Dulce said, *We're just puppies*

lying on our backs. Kofi asked, *But isn't the hatchet*
over the chicken's stretched neck—no matter how common
—always a surprise to the chicken? It had been a while
since we'd killed one so we had to think. *We're humanists,*
Albert said, *we don't believe in pestilence.*
Dirk told everybody to *please shut up* and take
a deep breath. Sofi reminded us that *pestilence*
or not, we apparently still believe in *petulance.*
Which got a laugh. Carelessness ensued.
We looked around the circle and saw others
we might have once wanted to have sex with,
and it blew our little minds. We began to pass
the salt without wiping our fingers. Sure, we've all
heard about the dying frogs. And certain whisperings
implicating bird men, forest dogs, and scofflaws. A few
true believers wander through the house warning us
to follow the rules, muttering dogma, or chirping
It's all still possible—all of it! Sometimes they scream
at the sky, so who can argue? And many
are secretly glad somebody still feels that way.
Even as our lights blink out, one by one—*willy-nilly,*
as most of us have come to believe. The helpful
or restless among us carry bodies and lay them
in the yard. Others load them on wagons heading
for the river. We're more organized than we've been
in a long time. It seems easier on the children.
They're always bothering us to play games.
They like hide and seek, but every time
one disappears, a parent shouts, *Why?*
over and over until it's hard to remember
anybody's face who isn't here anymore, or even
to bathe or eat, or do anything besides gaze at the weeping
willows we used to climb, trees we remember
being small, like us. *Chin up, chaps*, Colin might say.
And that helps. I mean, we make ourselves useful,
maybe sweep dead cluster flies off the windowsill
or disinfect door knobs. If you're wondering

about the guns, sure, they were shot. And we all
cleaned up the blood. Don said, *It's what people do,*
which felt important, and true. In the living room,
Adriana starts the movie and we join a group
on the couch. Something about bats, and locusts,
and thigh bones found in the desert. We can't
figure it out. Looks hot though. Lots of sun
and tigers, too. Pass the popcorn, somebody says,
and the popcorn gets passed. We stick our hands in,
lift our masks, and listen to each other chew.

Sharp Yellow Teeth

Regret

If everybody says
two lines are the same length
research shows
I do too.
And if I decide
to believe, then the light
over the mountain
proves it.
For as long as I've been alive
I used to think
that but now I know
this. Nevertheless
when my feet are on my desk
I can't help but assume
I'm right.
By the look in your eyes
you have legitimate gripes.
I kill, for example,
as naturally as I change
shirts and rehydrate.
In a body of proliferating
data streams
we need people around us,
but they're often wrong.
Ergo: Huckleberry Finn.
Ergo: Hester Prynne.
Mine say clean up:
get rid of the diapers and dishes and dog shit,
the unwanted children, the old
and crazy, inappropriate
and recently arrived;
the blunders of desire, the plastic, the mercury,
the blood of history. Me—
I drink it.
I like the messy
weight of it inside me.
I gulp from the fountain

until my belly bulges and I walk
gingerly. Still
I know
I should have picked up the phone
when I had the chance.

I'm a Spaceman

and where has it gotten me—
fierce and un-fallen
holding joystick
glory in a capsule
of my own making
—I'm
an engineer, as well—speeding
ten thousand miles an hour
not hiding from power
away from Earth
star-ward   yippee

it's not just gravity
I miss but the smell of it
the blue the blue the blue
backside shadow
deep as the sea of course
or women we men
buzz no matter how
old, like moths—
our irrelevancy patched
with money and big hats—
there's nothing and there's light
and everything else
the clouds below cover
men working in torture rooms—
oh sure
women too—
and the graves the graves under
dandelions and children
waving behind stone walls of broken homes
I wanted badly to live in

Aid

we run along the banks of a river
following a woman floating swiftly with the current
can you swim can you swim can you
swim   we shout

but we watch her head sweep along
until it's gone

we dive in and swim under ice
the water is cold and the current not easy
we see the woman, also a man and child
and pull them out
one by one and lay them on the bank
like cold white fish

wet and tired we realize we've saved no one
this disappoints us

*

at home, not *my home*
a wooden puppet, animated by dead parents
races through the house shouting and singing
loud! jumpy! crazy!

we grab its puppet arm and say   *hey*
hold it down yelling and kicking across our lap and say   *stop*

slowly the puppet turns into the drowned little boy alive
soaking wet
he grows calm, quiet
wow   we whisper   *a miracle*

the others crowd close and stare
as the boy begins to shiver and cry

*

don't leave   he whimpers
don't die
don't leave me

on and on like that

terribly moved we volunteer
our coats and cover him

don't die   he says
don't leave me

out the window sun shines
on green fields cut by blue water

we can't believe
how beautiful the world is

we won't   we say

Why I Don't Need Adrenaline-Rush Recreational Activities

Because despite my twin intentions of Awe
and Joy, dew-damp feet and warm manure
between my toes, I can't get the cows to go
where they need to go. I push but don't, push
but don't, and now I pull because the kitchen
door's stuck and somebody's pounding
and wants badly to get in. A pretty woman
taps my shoulder and hands me a drink. She tells me
we need to talk and something about her bracelets
makes me believe her. Because I'm waiting
in airport security and my team's already on the plane
but I forgot our money in the car. Outside
I meet an old friend whose name I should
but don't remember. The sun's in my eyes
and he asks about my dead parents
just as I get a question-mark text from somebody
on the plane. I don't know whom or how
to answer. Which rock to push and which
to sit on. And always with a little bit of the feeling
that maybe I'm talking too much. Certainly at the end
of the party, when my books come off the shelf. Nobody's
read them and everyone asks questions
I can't answer without making things up.
Kind of kills the party and a little something
inside me. But maybe the party's ending anyway
because the soccer game's over and I run
onto the field. My wife is being interviewed
by an African man in Spanish. She says something wrong
but clever and funny and we laugh. The grass is green
in that pretty way grass is green under lights.
She finishes and walks away. I'm calling
to get her to slow but the interviewer
catches my sleeve. I surprise myself at how
I can tell amusing stories in Spanish while searching
the crowd and trying to remember why.
I tell myself I'm okay. I tell myself

nobody knows why. I'm breathing in the same air
I'm talking out. In and out. I tell myself
for the time being nothing visible
will kill me. Because I'm hunkered behind a log
fingering my few remaining bullets while armed
men with chestnut boots and happy eyes
yip and weave around pink budding oaks.
Because I'm hot with summer and cold
under snow. Because the forest is endless
under a bright smear of stars. Because the moon's
grown heavy and can't last. Because all night long
it does.

Medicine

Sad and sick, I walked an empty street
in a foreign city past a gauntlet
of corner women taunting, and one screaming, *I want
to suck your cock!*—her words rising to fill the canyon
between buildings and falling down again —
all the way to the pharmacy.
On my return
I stopped and showed a tired but curious cluster
my hands cupped soberly around a little box
of medicine, and explained
my sleepless wife was ill
and waiting for me—*ever heard
a better excuse?* I turned and rode
the ripples of giggles behind me
until one woman's shout—*You don't even have
a dick to fuck with!*—was followed by tsunamis
of delight. Try to imagine breaking
laughter on all the empty streets of the world. Up
and down the carved facades of crumbling
buildings, washing sickness
and despair for just one bearable moment
bright, before only my footsteps on cobbles again
echoed against the blackened stone
as I turned down the alley pretending
to go home.

Needs

If men down here leave
body parts scattered in the jungle
to mark their law, the waves
will forgive them. New here,
you grumble into silence, bag
the pieces and send them home.
You wash your hands, put on clean
clothes and brush your hair.
Where the volcano's dark foot
dips into the sea, there's a small fire
to cook on. Wind turning the stars
and rattling zinc roofs
by dawn floats your mind
like a frigate bird—high and black
in the blue sky and still as morning
should be. You sit looking, limbs
cool from a swim. You haven't spoken
to anyone in days. Fishermen
bale flames of bloody water
over the side of their boat. A boy
drags a twisted stick past a girl with hair
black as burnt wood, past a manta ray
rotting on the beach, and you,
with your little books. Have you written
the lives you love?
The pig does *this,* the tiger *that*—
What do you need to do
to fly across the bay? What do you need
to die a little more
here, today?

Another October Sonnet

Head tangled in gray sky, feet
in rusty water, I eat a tomato and fancy
I'll take my clothes off, move to Mexico,
crawl the tracks through the *sala* to the *plaza*, swim
the fountain to the other side and climb out
eager and clean.

Here, I've smelled more fallen apples than I can count,
the curbs are heaped with leaves
again, and in the schoolyard each note
the band plays ends
in silence that makes me wonder
if anything will happen besides snow.

I always forget the sharp yellow teeth,
ad infinitum, of blue-eyed autumn.

Valentine's Day in the Mummy Museum

All the pretty girls
are dead
but the ones walking by.
I look at them
arrogant with life
and frightened in the dark.
The dead,
who might have used dying
to build character,
are silent.
What was it—
this one asked as she died—
that so darkened our world?
Skin shriveled to paper, still with hair,
eyeless behind glass.
Or she may have whispered
with disappearing lips,
Life is hard!
You have to drink
so much water every day.
Or maybe, Life is beautiful
and this is not how I used to look.

For now
let's stand in the corner
and touch cheeks.
(I'll imagine yours.)
Care for me, I'll ask,
in all the small, absurd ways.
Show me empty shoes
and dirty socks and yesterday's pants
under the bed,
and no monster
waiting to drink my blood.
Feed me
ice cream from your spoon.
The walls are brittle, the floor cracked.

It's afternoon and past the last chamber,
out the door,
the sun we love
is dying too.

Success

I wake with a beautiful idea sliding
through my fingers—something about seagulls?
By the time the first drops from the sun-lit
icicles fall from the eves, it's a hummingbird

then a horse that just last night in the snow
left tracks across the yard. Somewhere
along the race there's a red mare with eyes wet
as spring breathing steam from her nostrils.

I try to hold her where she is. From the glazed
but still green grass on the bench two doe
whistle and I ask them to help. They stare
down long faces as if to say: our people

don't do that—then they run away.
How do they know it'll all end badly?

San Pedro Sula

Gangsters roam the last night on earth,
falling as it does, where she is, too,
no phone, like the old days when I dropped
into a hole and no one knew. What else
but love under a sky heavy enough to crush, and me
on rusted bedsprings, with beer and soccer on TV.
I wonder if she's warm, if the frozen lake
will hold, if wind snaps the sparks
of her fire toward the stars. Here mountains
turn to ghosts that mumble in the hall,
and I leave salt sheets to walk past tangled squatters,
sea-sighs of invisible women, a happy bowman
hunting sparse boulevards for the blink
of distant light. Nothing says good morning
like gunshots at dawn, and she, her feet in snow,
steps past pine and hemlock toward a cold car
she hopes will start. Snowflakes
sparkle on pastel, and skin burns to believe
air is water, the cracked sidewalk
a coral reef. Beauty swims mute with ugly, and I,
big with both, feel the roll of their affection
make new words for old things to say.

Solitude

Now it's only you
and your idea
of time alone
but time moves
slowly and sometimes
you shiver with it
or it heats your head
until your brain boils
and your idea
has disappeared
behind the chair—
no one's there—
and whatever hope
you might have had
fled with the night
and the moon
that lit the table
where she kept her things
by the bed
empty of all but shadow
your breath
the sound of dogs
while you wait to see
what happens next.

Soon It Will Be Later

Maybe This Time

This way, you say, through those doors
over the line, our papers stamped—
that must mean something. When in doubt,
breathe, take your seat with the rest
of the hunters and thieves.

The people here are different—
not just their hats—they know nothing
of the ashes behind us, the sad
world we've invented or how far we have
left to go. It's warmer, blue around the bend.
Volcanoes bind the bay on the other side—
another place we've never been. I should
have kissed you more, made a home
safe from tigers.

Maybe this time, you say. The breeze
is fair—pelicans soar and fall
and float like boats. It's afternoon
on an endless day. Across the sand,
waves of heat turn light to dream, and I—
for a step or two—believe you.

Blue

Under a cupped-hand sky thirty feet
over a quarry pool in the deep north
of childhood—who in that big middle
is on your side? You want so much
so badly all you can do is jump. Falling,
you watch iron ridges hump the horizon
north to the arctic. Nothing ends, it seems.
Yet halfway down over the flat
eye of water you understand: everything
in your short life has. Crystal shatters
when you hit and comes together again
as you sink. You never felt a blue
so cold or true and won't again until you rise
and gasp the sky. Some things
you don't want stay with you, but this—
wherever water holds you—
will too.

Toil

Everything I feel
I've forgotten makes me stuff
other lives into the hole
of mine, slide old cars
down cutbanks for riprap,
dump sacks of bones
to fill the slough or flat out
invent a rock in the swamp
to stand on. So the work
continues.

Flying

My life's a series of trips
I forget between looking
for keys. Even if I know
they're in my pocket, a quick
touch helps. Which
brings me to what I won't do
to feel less anxious: Very
little. After all these years
I'm still afraid of being locked out
in the rain, mercilessly
beaten, called a racist
(because it's true)
told to please shut up
(because I ought to)
—and even worse
—shutting up and dying a coward.
I worry but it's never enough.
Out the window under a wing
and heavy sky there's always
a dead man on the runway, suitcase
open, dollar bills flocking
in the breeze. For fortitude
I remind myself when I say *always*
I'm usually wrong and sometimes
I wish I were young but not as often
as I used to be afraid I'd never write
a good novel or touch a beautiful woman. Turns out
the dollar bills are crows, the dead
man an empty sack, and the lucky ones
temporarily strapped in our seats, sipping drinks
and feeding our children. Live
long enough and all myth turns
prayer. If I ever get home I'll peel
myself inside out and dance
on the table. I'll beg
to clean the fridge. Eat better.
Vote.

My Country Loved Me

The horses my god how
they could have crushed our feet and bit
our hands but only lipped
sugar from our palms
and gaped to show tremendous
tongues—and the cats too
how they walked rail fences
pausing to sit on posts
hunting mice in grass or snow—and sometimes
it seemed the horses regarded the cats
and the cats regarded the horses
as I regarded both:
beautiful in blizzards or rain or heavy
green sickening heat of July or cool
morning August fog, shadows
and hooves I could feel
through my mattress at night, eyes rolling
and steam rising from wet
backs solid as the smell of the tack
that touched them hanging
in a darkened room.

In boy dreams I'm their equal
still, their flesh mine—
pregnant Black Kitty again leaps
from her box into my bed and scratches
my leg as she pushes out
the first of four kittens—or old Bob
with the broad back
who quiets as I climb on and walks me
to the pond where he twitches
flies and waits while I swim and fill
my stringer with bass, waits like a gray uncle
to take me home again.

Waiting for Breakfast

On the wire across the road against
A gray sky, sneakers hang, and under them a man
Stumbles home from a drunk past
A child walking with her hood up and hand
On her scarfed Grandmother's arm.
What else is there? whistles
The clarinero—two notes sliding upward over
And over again from its perch
On the roof—what else is there besides
Wheelbarrows in relation to chickens
And a cactus standing stoic in the yard?

Well there's this:
My twitchy memory of an odd and erotic
Dream, a gnawing unease in my belly, dogs
Barking through the fence about health
Care and immigration reform, and if
I'm not mistaken, details on how to simplify
The tax code. Also
There's an invisible chill in the breeze
That comes from somewhere I've never been
And goes to somewhere I've yet to go.

So if you're asking, strange orange-eyed
Black bird, if these relations, one visible thing
To another, are precious?
They are. But if you're asking
If they're all there is, well
I hope not. It's morning
And a little patch of blue sky grows in the east
And in the west fog pours through the green
Gap like pea soup and of course
I'm imagining things: A bird
Asking the same questions as I do, a warmer
Afternoon, perhaps, and the imminent
Arrival of breakfast.

Not Quite Fall

Hollyhocks, pink shimmers north of the road
over blurred yellow grass, a smatter
of red sumac and still green oak hedging
the field make me stop the car and get out.

I stand and lean. The only thing moving
is rising from reeds and shadow stacks
of hay among Van Gogh flowers: what my
brother and I named *Aug,* too long ago,

what fairies leave when night flees in August,
when dew bejewels spider silk and the ground
turns to mist that again veils the valley
like a fall bride. What did we know? What we

needed, I suppose. I listen to summer
birds discuss winter. One, then another.

For a Boy I Knew and Read about in the Newspaper

If your death made the heavens
brighter, I'd thank you
for sacrificing yourself on a full-speed, full-stop
collision with a tree,
rather than curse your dumb ass
for not even wearing a helmet.
But alas, it won't. My anger
turns the moon red—
another thing you'll never see again, or Mars
blinking over the mountain like a beacon
or a warning.

Twenty years old and the world
excited you to sexy, fit, badass, hardcore—
your words. Where else
but standing full speed under a thin opening of stars
long-boarding on blacktop through the forest
do they make sense?
Don't the stars shimmer and shadows beckon
all the dumb young men
who want to die with their boots on? The ones
who haven't yet learned
you haven't lived—as my old man used to say—
until you've been laid with them off?
The ones who dive from cliffs to know
the water's depth, ski couloirs or speed
curves to find out if they're brave enough
to save themselves and the ones they love—
who need them only to grow up and learn to walk
across a meadow shimmering
        (there's that word again)
into the August shadow of a mountain sloped
        (sweetness comes, it does)
toward the dusting of new snow.

They'll say you loved the feel of night air on your hair—
well, we all do—
as though that makes everything okay,
feeling what you loved, doing and dying that way.
But the paper said you lay broken that long night
on the forest floor and died face-down in the morning.
Which twists me to think about: how
you opened your eyes and saw
not dawn spreading past tree tops
but dank leaves and dark loaming
through shadow past shadow to the empty place,
where music began and loss sprouts
mystery bliss and the same cold dreams
        to wake, to fly
that bloom in my own bed of sorrow each morning,
just before I open mine.

The Newlyweds Next Door

They ski across the lake into the storm
and the sting of tiny flakes
until—what?—their hearts beat madly

in the wind that begins across the flat
of the world and rattles
my window—their edges dim

shapes grow small—
not really rattles
because the house is solid and the window is big and my room

warm and from here I watch
as their figures become one and slip
blind into the blizzard.

Now I can only imagine
or remember the snap of snow against their coats
and lungs burning and the sound

of skis and lights from shore
gone in the white roar.
Now it's only they and their bodies

and their world narrowed
to just a few yards wide
where they stop

to catch their breaths and shout
gleefully to each other and hear their voices
swirl, where they turn

and turn some more, tracks blown over—how
will they know
which way to go?

But they don't go yet.
For as long as they can
they feel their smallness fill the world

and yes, this is where their hearts begin to ache
gladly, blown madly loose and tucked
down into the joy

into the pull of it, into the wild light
weight of it. Then with the wind at their backs in the middle
of the lake, they begin to ski again.

They can't believe how fast they fly.
Through watery eyes
they watch for ghost

trees and yellow lights
on shore, gliding
full speed toward a home they trust

with animal heat to be where they left it
where they imagine it to be.
I wait for them to reappear—

a face at the window floating
in time and lost
in white. I wait and disappear

until two in one—there, a tiny figure
from a dream—
I resurrect as they do.

Now What

There was no rip
and wild fall.
We lay down, remember?
There's frost on the hay—
we're on our backs,
the blue sky
harder than we thought,
the river grayer
than it's ever been.
A canyon wind swirls panic,
leaves and ecstasy.
It's afternoon—
but who can tell?
September. The race
is dry. I wait
for what I've done to name
what I think I'll be.
And if it does,
if I do, perhaps I'll feel
myself again.
Or lacking that,
we'll build a boat.
Up high there's snow, and the geese
can't make up their minds.

As a General Rule

If I find a slanting spot of sun
On stone steps between
Morning shadows
Under a giant
Bronze lion
After a many-monster
Night
When my feet hurt
And it's January fifth
Again
I sit

Soon
It will be later

Things We Say

Whatever Happened to Them?

(ten couples we used to know)

1

He was embarrassed to be caught
without candles
on her birthday
or matches
so he rubbed two sticks together
to light himself on fire.
She watched flames lick up his legs and higher
to his neck and face and her cool hands
touched his burning ones
and they lived for a moment
like that.

2

Like turtles on a log
they sat next to each other all season
until one day she stepped forward and plopped
into the pond and swam away.
He watched her fade into the murk, and grieved
for he'd never seen the bottoms
of her feet before
and he couldn't yet imagine
his life alone, or how the log beneath him
sloped from the grassy bank down
to touch both water and sky.

3

After he left her
he slid women like rings
over his penis, each large
then shrinking
to make room for the next
until, fever past, his body

faded like a clear idea
and only a smile-shaped
string of plastic dolls connected
one dark planet eye
with the other

4

Perhaps they never forgave each other
for sneaking so close
but didn't they say, *Please please
please?*
Didn't they tear off their clothes
and jump each other?
Or maybe they bumped their heads
and forgot
how they began: bobbing
at sea with voluptuous hope.
Wind! Lightning! Big waves!
Fun! For soon they tired, searched
for calm, stared across endless water and thought
about throwing each other overboard
and how they used to be
nice people.

5

When the chaos got too much for her
she sat on his head and absorbed him.
For a while we heard
shrieks between her thighs
but he quieted and she
did too, her skin and bones
drying to dust over
the shape of a tiny man
fetal inside her.

6

He opened the old door
and she followed him up stone
ramps built centuries ago for horses and heroes,
around and around, breathless past slits like green
eyes opening to olive groves farther
and farther below. When the sky finally
swept blue around the last corner
she saw over the rooftop terrace
and a spread of land fuzzy with heat
the distant line of the sea.
He kissed her, climbed
onto the wall, paused, his skinny arms birdlike,
and jumped. For the rest of her life
she watched him fall.

7

The morning she told him
in too many words why she was leaving,
he disappeared into silence.
Air filled his shirt and pants.
His empty shoes looked particularly sad
under the table.
When she finally walked out, she left a paper bag
with her heart in it.
He was too afraid to look
and for a long time
hungry, while he finished his coffee
he was hoping it was scones.

8

Because she was planted
among split rocks and ashes—
tended with winter and spite

in the draughty rubble
of the old church—her daisy
grew iron-stemmed, spindly
and brave—oh so brave—
toward the faintest flicker
of sun. From the damp
among peonies he watched,
molted and—oh so moved
—only waited.

9

When one plate of the earth's crust
slid under another
their pretty house crumbled.
Covered in mud, they snarled
and crawled into their own
separate dark caves, where they re-invented fire
and sleep under fur. We hear
they're happy now.

10

Dancers, they made themselves
beautiful shapes and circled
each other, touched and leaned
until their bodies became one.
A pretty bird
fluttered down from the sky
and landed on their shoulder.
For as long as they could, they strained
to hold still.
But one of them moved and the other fell
and the bird flew away.
Years later they woke to hear feathers
ruffling in the dark near their ears. Faces close,
they kissed,
for they knew it wouldn't stay.

What I Want

Inside all day. Rosalie's gone
to monastery. On most mornings yellow
makes the air look new but today
it's thunder gray, Packers on the radio, and cold
blows through the open doors that look out
over the old city. Ate chicken
and *ji-tomate* for lunch. (Who knew?
Turns out the *pendejo* Spanish stole the fruit
and changed the name.) Finished
Gone with the Wind and can't believe
I care about stupid, selfish, racist
Scarlet, but I do. I want Rhett to love
her again. I want Mellie and Bonnie
alive. I want somebody to care. I want
what's done to be undone. I want kindness
and no regrets. I don't like broken things.
I want the bad calls reversed. I want
all the perfumes of Arabia to sweeten Lady
Macbeth's bloody hands. I want the spot
out, too. I want it gone. Don't you?

People Are Saying

Dogs are love, and goats are
aliens, and some say their grandmothers visit
as ponies, and if you've never
heard that before, well
now you have—you've heard it, too.
We've all heard
a ghost in the basement and the Mongols
are coming and Africans
are liars and the technology's faster
every day, and sometimes
it's true.

That's what I've heard.

A lot of people are saying
money is worth something, we all agree
but not as much as we thought,
and this painting costs more than all the houses
on your block, and that man with gold teeth
emptied the lake and built a casino
for his dead daughter
so he could buy the painting and
build a track for his wife's ponies
and I've heard it's going to get worse
before it gets better.

You've heard it, too. It's gone viral.

People are saying they believe in spheres
or crystals, and you gotta want it.
People are saying you didn't want it bad enough
or he wanted it too much
and she should have known better
and he should have known more
and kept his mouth shut and she should have
not kept her mouth shut or posted the picture
if it bothered her so much and

when the warm weather melts the glaciers
it's all God's fault, people are saying
maybe or maybe not, or it's all your fault
for being born where you were born
and for driving your car to work and to get
groceries and for staying warm in your house
and flying to see your grandma the pony.

I'm just saying, people are asking.

Who are we to say anything
given who people say we are
since mom died owing money and dad ditched
to the north, in fact we better
pay up, they say
even if we didn't buy the house or the drugs or the polo
ponies grandma loved so well. People are saying
it's all her fault for having seventeen children
which is why they say
we need a purge
we need to suffer for the sins of our fathers—you see
people are starting to believe
in purity.

That's what they say, have you heard that?

And purity is power and
no-power is everybody wondering
if you're pure enough, and I've heard
people say we're not—or you aren't
anyway—
in fact a lot of people are saying
maybe you should just say you're sorry
you're sorry, so everybody can hear
you're sorry.

That's what I've heard. You've heard it now, too.

Nothing and *absolutely* are a couple of words
a lot of people are saying—
as in *nothing*
is certain, *absolutely*, but what we believe
and people are saying women can be men
and men can be women, and anybody
can make love with anybody as long as they do it
between this line here
and that line there, and only after
certain words I've heard, and you have, too
are spoken
sounds made with our mouths
sounds our mothers taught us
mean certain things, everybody agrees
except those who had different mothers
or stubbornly say maybe or maybe not
or say they don't or can't understand the sounds
or don't mean those things when they say
those words
or just have trouble hearing.

People are saying.

They're asking, what about god
and love and peace
and what happens when others
with different hats
ride over the hill on horses, or on metaphoric horses
and start crossing the line, people are saying
everybody says, everybody believes
is there
between this wooden stake
and that one, between yours absolutely
and mine. Some people say
people who say maybe or maybe not
will need to be shot
and others say

nobody knows
but Nobody might be anybody.

I've heard that story, we all have.

People are saying the border
used to be there
but now is here even though some people
refuse to believe it and others are saying—
and you've heard this too, or now you have—
we need to follow
that guy with the boots, absolutely, or give
our children to that one with the drum
on the corner
because a lot of people are saying
the world is full of horror—they keep filling
baskets with chopped-off heads
both real and metaphoric—
also the everyday suffering of the old
or the cold
wet and sick, the grieving and alone, who tiptoe past
rain puddles or blood puddles
trying to remember
or to pronounce the name
of their new street.

Just saying.

A lot of people are saying
they were happier when they lived
on the mountain, metaphorically speaking
they had better rain gear
and everybody had a great car and cooked over a fire
that never went out, and now they're saying
we're all going to die, absolutely
but other people are saying maybe
or maybe not, because wouldn't it

be something if everybody started believing
we'll all come back
as ponies?

I'm just saying, people are saying.

It's a long way to Tipperary, and from what I've heard
we'll never get there
so we better get busy and invent
our virtue
regardless of the evidence.
It could be just like money
or the value of money
how we could we make it true
our goodness by fiat
if we all believed
and tortured anybody who didn't, just in case
like people say, and you've heard too
we already do.

American Innocence

Our people
used to use your people
as stools—for our feet, sure, but also
to sit on your bare backs and rest.

Our flatulence
made us shake with laughter.
What else could we do?
It must have been unpleasant but

Our people were shit on
by these people—or was it
those?—when they weren't busy
slaying our brothers.

We don't like them.
But your people we always admired.
We were boys—we felt safe at last.
Our bottoms were on your backs.

Tragic Heroes

Won't stop thinking or wanting or running or
jumping or fighting or dreaming so much

Or stop with the drugs already
and the boozing and sexing

And speeding toward the abyss everybody
sees but them

Then falling and making me think *there
but for the grace—*

And wonder what I can't see right in front of my face.

Why can't they be more like me or who
I think I am or want to be—

Superman, say, or other guys who fly
and don't crash

Or do but don't die
and make me love in smoky ruins

Their broken bones
their pissed-on roses

And my own peculiar, inevitable demise.

Red, White, and Blue

There's an American I am
who thinks the world is his oyster
because he ate it

who feels sorry for himself
because he's full

who'd like to change
by changing the world

he's thinking, *tool*
I just need the right goddamn tool

There's an American I am
who feels virtuous
when others aren't

who seals his doubts
in a barrel to stand on

who shines his face
until he forgets them

he's thinking, *me*
I'm absolutely sure about me

There's an American I am
who thinks if he only wants it bad enough
he'll be beloved

dressed in mountain chic
a horse between his knees

he's buried to his eyeballs
in his own language

thinking, *free*
at least I'm fucking free.

We Are Not the Chosen Elves

they are someone else
we are in the green room waiting
trying to keep from hating
the others and their mothers
who walk on stage as stars, seen finally as who they are

when no one ever knocks, we drift outside
around the block, past strangers like us
getting off the bus, and the ones we used to be
(who swim with manatees!) and the girls along the pier
still waiting to hear—

squinting through the ether, they don't see us either

apparently not a visible pair, we don't worry about our hair
we shuffle under almond trees and frigate birds
past soccer games and human turds
and colored chalk on cracked sidewalks
to a skiff on the beach that we steal

(like a peach!) and row along the shore

after the sun flares red, a drunken promise
before bed, and the last swinging torch
blinks out on a porch, the bubbles in our wake
light like sparklers (on a cake!) and the plaint of our oars
turns the stars—

our voices over water, somebody's son
somebody's daughter

Self-Made Man

He stood barefoot night
and day for years and conducted
until his arms ached the waves
to curl and crash and spread
one after another up the beach.
Often he'd be hungry and tired
and sad and lonely but kept
it up so long and well he's proud
to say that when he got old, he had only
to leave explicit instructions
for the waves to continue.

Young French Lovers Are No Better Off
Than Any Other Kind

Shadow and sunshine are equally shy
across the faces of the young French lovers
on the bench in the plaza near the Callejón de Besos.
The wind cools the sweat on their brows but raises
some uncomfortable questions: like where did they go—
those warm moist smells that held them close? Even their breath
floats away with the shouts of children and clusters
of red balloons.

Her nostrils below absurdly large sunglasses flare
as they did last night, when fully-submerged in her,
he lifted her off the bed and — clinging to his neck
and waist as he carried her onto the balcony and down—
she came again and again with each step
down the stairs and across the beach until the sea climbed her legs
to her chest and neck, and the two of them floated
apart like jellyfish.

He's sprawled on the plaza bench like a crucified Christ,
arms spread, legs straight and ankles crossed,
eyes closed and face to the fickle sun. The ground rumbles
beneath the cobbles. He wonders what she remembers, if
she remembers, and where they are now. He wonders
about a cigarette and where the tunnels go. She looks past
the cluster of shops to the sky so blue it wants to assume her—
is that the word? Or it already has—and she's hanging up there
like that passing cloud, pretty and strange, impaled
on the steeple.

Hungry? he says, and looks at her.

With lovers, even young French lovers,
there are no questions but meaningless ones, and all
the answers are meaningless as well.
A stray lock blows across the swell of her lips, across a face
that betrays in stillness everything irrepressible

and equivocal in her desire. Soon men might jump
from planes and steer parachutes for the plaza, bombs
explode and a truck roar past trailing smoke,
but in their perfect state of unknowing, his and hers,
of never knowing, there's only this
that matters—
when she turns her face to his.

The Mysterious Location of Kyrgyzstan

Who

Some people fall in love only once
and some never, and some like Elizabeth Taylor
or my Great Aunt Edna with a parade of lovers—
a wood cutter to whom she whispered into his sawdust
beard, *I'm a plant and your kisses the rain*, a dough-handed baker
whose warm bread made her cry
a merchant marine with a tattooed belly who woke
nightly trembling and gasping into her ear.
And some fall in love
with the same person over and over
for decades, and each time say the same
common, sacred things.

What

The workers at the post office
in Addis Ababa
can't take my daughter's letter
to her friend in Kyrgyzstan
because they say they don't know
where that country is.
She shows them a map
but still they shake their heads.

When

In the morning with coffee and the evening under
a half moon and when we're born and when
we wake in the middle of the night and don't know
where we are. When the bus drops us off where two dirt
roads cross in the jungle and it rains and we sing
until the bus finally comes and we climb wet and steaming
through the door and settle on top of our bags and sleep.
When we get where we're going and before we get there

when we're hungry and thirsty and tired and can't sleep
and we look down and see dolphins next to the boat
or the light in the water the color of sky past snow-covered fir.
When we see our children born and our parents die
and we lay the ashes of a child in a grave and later laugh
and look at beautiful women and eat dessert. When the beer
is gone and the band has finished playing and we walk home
through a maze of alleys and up and down a thousand stairs
to lie finally in our beds and listen to the breath of a buffalo
outside our tent or our window, or the voice of a dead boy
or the wind, the unending wind.

Where

After pointing to the closest trotting
street dog and asking the closest person
where that dog is going
hundreds of times in various Honduran towns
during a six-year research period
and never getting another answer other than a shrug
my scientist brother concludes that nobody knows
where the Honduran streets dogs are going.

Why

Because our lovers are strong and kind
and because they are cruel and weak and because we are everything
they are including jealous & thrilled & disgusted
& scared, and when we love
we feel all those things and also happy
& sad but despite our confusion
we know why we suffer
why we die, why we eat and sleep and why
we wake and what we mean
when we say the common, sacred
things we say.

Baskets of Purple Garlic

You Could Have Had Me

Outside your door under the streetlight
Up the hill
On the steps by the restaurant

                              Below the church.

And I, you.
There's a moment when it can go either way—a ball
Off the wall
A raindrop on the divide—and it always does.

                              Eternity

We invent
So we don't fall off the lobe of now. Still
It's music I like
The echoing howl of everything I did and everything

                              I didn't do.

I'm imagining things,
You say, and of course you're right, but isn't
That the glory?
The best we can do? I'm done writing

                              Obituaries

Can't pretend to glide
Around the back of death and hold close with full sadness
The truth.
This hallowed air

                              Is ours for now

The pull of blood a sweet slide to yes
Or a just-as-joyful
No.
Just so you know, I've taken to floating on the pond at night

                              My cock a lily

Chest an empty
Turtle shell without you. When I climb out
Dripping
I roll in sand and breathe down stars,

                              A hundred thousand

Leaves, your fingers and hair,
An entire cloud. Then I close my eyes and smell precious
Failure,
Feel on my skin the electric rain

                              Of bewilderment,

Each rise and fall of my chest, a first and last

                              Happy breath.

Good Luck

Once my heart burst
me out of sleep and urged me run across
the river (or swim—I did that, too) and knock
on a girl's door. I had nothing but my desire—

no words, not even breath—so I kissed her
and she kissed me back, and the rest makes little sense
as well. Now I'm alone by a fire, drunk with the blood
that made me, dancing under the same stars

that made and turned millions, now all dead.
It's just a way to keep from feeling alone.
I can hear my dad if I told him. Easily
amused but kind, he took my ambitions

seriously. In his last years his boyhood loneliness
returned, and he sat looking at things he couldn't
understand, pictures, rings, pages of writing,
my mother. Good luck, he'd say, with all that.

Morning People

We like everything
to go according to plan
and when it doesn't—
we hope that somehow everything's
connected to a bigger plan
because if it's not—
and we're left standing on the plains at nightfall
in a big wind with hands in our pockets—
aren't we fools again?

We know sometimes
it's the same Great Notion
that hoists magnificent stones and builds a great pyramid
as destroys a city and makes ashes of children—
and that doesn't help.

The fatigue, dear me—
as we lie in our beds at night
protecting ourselves from a painful past
and groping for what—
we don't even know what—
we lost back there.

What do we need to do
to be happy? To be grateful for what is
and to dream of better?

Stare at the ceiling and listen
to the lunatic bird in the yard,
feel, in the stillness that follows,
furry despair, his unblinking eyes
on our skin that changes as we sleep,
strangely, to a vast stretch of beach
lined with palm trees, a sky, a boat,
a sea so clear the stone dropping from our fingers
falls forever into emptiness.

Then, because we can—
because somewhere past where we can see
we hear a dog bark, the drip
of a faucet or the song of a man selling avocados—
we lean toward shore
put on our traveling hats
tilted just so
to give us that jungle cool.
That's right, we step out—

Doesn't the light delight?
Last night, uncountable cruelties—
but today?

The Purpose of Kissing

Ever notice how the smallest
words uttered between lovers
are attached to boulders
too high up the mountain
to see? A syllable
can shake one loose and send
it tumbling to crush flesh and bone
and the lives of children.

Think of it like this: lovers
hold tiny detonation devices
on their tongues, hot invisible
wires attached to distant charges
strategically placed.

But if that's true, then how
do they breathe? How do
they speak at all?

Maybe like this: First
we look into each other's
eyes and slowly our faces
approach until we touch
our lover's most dangerous place
with our most dangerous place.

We kiss to breathe. We kiss to talk.
If we're still alive, we kiss some more.

A Very Short History of Things

This brings me to how it's going
to go—what I should have said
in your arms last night
when you asked: First we'll try
to climb into each other's skin again, with some
success, and then we'll think
and talk real hard: *Thinkthink
talktalk.*   Feel.   Yuck.
Which is to say a day will pass
or two. Scorched and dumb
we'll walk to the end of the block
to where the Asian—they say Asia's
a big country—has made a new device
that brings the bison back
and tricks us into believing
well-used guns will make it safe
to start campfires again. Marshmallow
sales will go bonkers.

Oh sure, sons will disappear
as they often do, and the anger
of daughters will turn them away
as well. Hearts will always find
new ways to break but the mending
will be sweeter. Imagine the river
full of fish again, or men sailing boats
with snow north and south
to rebuild the icecaps.

If that sounds like too much
remember we'll soon be dead. Still
you'll be glad to know
working under orange trees and drunk
on citrus again, we refused
to die embittered and the earth indeed
bothered with our bones. What I'm trying
to say is there's still time to embrace

our failure and let our own dirt
assume us, time for lilacs
to make our late arrival
trivial to springtime.

Here lies another with another
someone might say.
Not the first, or the last.

For the Uncountable Time

since we've been children
                    we heard the president say
we're bombing people there

and people here cheer
or stare through windows
                    or sleep
through the news.

Soon we'll be alone on the playground
pounding our chest and shouting
                    We're free! We're free!
We're free!

to the two or three left standing.
Wind. Sky. Stars.
                    Then silence.
What's a little unease here

when the cliffs up there
are a hundred million years old?
                    Lately
even the simplest things you say

open my heart.
See the yellow leaves—
                    I do.
(I drop to my knees.)

—blow across the grass?
I do.
                    I do.
Are we saved

by predestination
or by choices we've made?
                    Nobody knows
and everybody has an opinion

like a navel
we touch from time to time
                    lest we forget
how sunshine explodes

trees in green and where perhaps
we stand on that.
                    Wind and rivers
come from somewhere we only imagine

and go
to another place we only imagine
                    which is why we love them so.
Apple blossoms carpet the brick

like feathers
and then—when?
                    the apples ripen and fall and mush
for the wasps

and then—when?
they turn to soil for roots to grow in.
                    Potatoes. With butter.
We're a lot of little people

with a lot of little powers
and we'll be gone
                    sure enough
one way or another.

Those we've been bombing
might even bomb us back.
                    Luck, after all

needs an explanation

only when it's bad.
It's October
                    and I'm still in love with things
that won't hold still:

rivers, clouds
the stripe of light

                    across my desk
and you.

On a Cliff with You

If we were both
hanging from a cliff
by one hand
you'd tell me how scary
it was to be hanging
from a cliff
by one hand
and we'd talk about
how it made you feel
and how your hand
hurt
and how the sun
was setting.

I'd be wondering
how long
I could endure
and we'd talk
about how long you thought
you could endure
and then
you'd tell me everything
you'd learned
about enduring
as long as you had.

I'd listen and watch
night fall
until you suddenly noticed
me hanging
and praised my heroic endurance
and said how ashamed
you felt
to have talked
so long
when I was suffering too.

I'd say that's OK
and you'd say it wasn't
and I'd say OK
it wasn't
and you'd laugh
and we'd both be silent
hanging
in the dark.

Then
just when I'd think
I could not hold on
another moment
you'd find a ledge
to put your feet on
and I don't know how
but you'd help me find it too.

We'd let ourselves down
together
and sit safely
on the ledge
under the stars
dangling our legs.

Luna

Down the gravel drive, the porch light a golden
pin on the black valley swirling with what I tried
to say as we got out and slammed the car doors,
how I could never trust the answers and people
who gave them. Spring, like us, was noisy with hope
and smothered with growth we hadn't a clue what
to do with. How could we know how long the past
would last? We might have lain on the grass, quiet
beyond imagined children or the prematurely
dead, felt the rain sublime the ground
beneath us, or locked ourselves inside and made
the scratchy, squeaky sounds of mice. Instead
you pointed at the broken yellow door
and the moth flat against the screen and pale
green, the size of a bird or a painted hand
left by a moon man. We paused and breathed, and stopped
our incessant talking. All philosophy grows
from suffering what to make of this beauty
with no more than a week to live. Was she waiting
for her mate to fly into that fierce wind?
Or maybe the moth was a he and he was staying
for her. Nothing to lose but slippery convictions,
I stood still. Everything
I've tried to say since, I've tried to say
from there.

You and Me and the Dead

A pain before I move
of air and time and the apple
of jazz bouncing out the door
among shouts of invisible children,
also death or not-me, and the un-kissed face
of the girl—the light a blanket
over her shoulders—
make the day ache enough
to last forever.

A poem flew by last night.
I heard it in the air when I looked up
and saw the North Star for the first time
in a long time, on my way home
in an alley I've walked a thousand times.
The earth is flat, the sky streaked with red wings.
If I'm this close to the edge
is there room for anything else?

It's a thing I've danced
around and pointed to, but have no clue
what's really there. A streetlight, a dog
waiting by the door, an empty
table, a clean ashtray, a woman
writing in a book, the curve of her neck
an invitation to receive. The moon
is in every poem, but there it is again
hanging over the biggest city
on this side of the earth, and a man
cleaning his car sings a love song
written by somebody dead, for somebody
only imagined.

Before we were here, they were.
They liked having lunch and their
nails done. They smoked pipes and took
long walks. Some had three wives

as was their custom, some had none, and some shared
husbands or had one and lived in a house made of hides
or mud and hunted with sharp rocks, painted
their skin, talked to the sky or the earth
or invisible animals, chewed coca and staked
hairless enemies to the ground.
Some thought cats were gods, or dogs were, or virgins
and others kept people as pets, grabbed them
and copulated willy-nilly.
Many were fun and happy and many
miserable and not good company.
When they greeted each other
they bowed to the earth or grabbed each other's testicles
if they had them, or touched noses
if they didn't, or breasts. Some
were very important and others weren't
and were slaughtered
because they lived on the other side of the river
or down in the valley.
Women came with cows, or were available for purchase
if a man had cows, but there were a lot of men and women
with no cows, and they came, too
if they were asked
or whenever they wanted to. Sometimes
they loved—
did I mention that?—as we do. Sitting
late at night they put their chins in their palms
and listened.
They held hands and rested
on each other's shoulders, whispered
dear in their own dear breath. Now
they're all dead and this is our clear
light, our poem, and the day
aches enough. We're both
still here.

What with Light We Might Imagine

Before dawn, you greet hotel maids
chatting music, step around dog shit
on the clean cobbled walk past garbage
trucks and taxis in the cold. After
a long night of righteous missiles
over the holy land, the last echo of *¡puta
madre!* has dissolved down the block
and the fairy glow of streetlights guides
you toward a paling sky, Cinco de Mayo
and coffee.

Still squinting from the glare on the Santa Martha
bus, you walk into the shade past armed
guards on broken chairs and the same
one who blocked your way to leave that first
afternoon, said it's too late, you'll have to stay
the night inside. Remember the dark
in your throat, the sudden glint in his eye,
a prison joke. Ha-ha.

Hunched over pencils, beige-clad men
turn their attentive faces you won't have
enough time to get to know. Your afternoons
fill with the broad light on a hundred Rivera
murals, the glow of surrealist women
at Chapultepec, the dapple through trees
in the Condesa, watching Obama win
on plasma TV, three-course lunches at clean
shadowed counters just one sane step
out of the glare. You blow your mind wondering
how many minds the Cathedral's enormity
has blown before yours, and did all those people
also walk out the back door, cross the street
and buy their first suit for their living mother's
funeral? Your wife suggests you bought it
for your own. You climb curving hotel
steps past a wide glass floor lit

from below and posted with potted plants
squeeze in the dim elevator with Italians
close your eyes and savor the top of a pretty
woman's dark head. All that so you know
you'll never remember their names: *Oscar,*
Luís, Perpetuidad and three dozen more.
While walking long prison hallways past men
selling food, smoking, playing handball
against concrete walls, standing, laughing
or squatting with hands covering their faces
you know you've only dipped your toes
and stared over yet another endless sea.

But what more can you do? Raised
a thousand miles from the ocean, at twenty
you wrote your first poem stunned by sparkle
and how the same water touching your feet
touched every shore on earth, the prows
of Greek and Viking ships, and all the feet
of all the people who stood and stared
since the beginning of time. Wow, you
thought. Wow.

You're still saying it. Remember the cab
in the rain, the drops on the glass bend light
and time, one block after another, this strange
unending city fills the creeks and bathes the plains
of your dry old mind. Wet pavement wafts
through the cracks and your mouth waters
at the thought of your wife happy after a week
at the monastery. You remember the Bar Odessa
and your younger self at the Café La Blanca
touched by the beauty and her note
you began another story—maybe the first
decent story you ever wrote and pure
imitation. You lean your head on cool glass
watch couples stroll the Alameda dangling

cigarettes and jewelry, sex and spring—well
you're making that up, but why not—
which leads you to think of pyramids
built without wheels or beasts, the city floating
on a lake—how many stones carried from where
to fill it?—and that's only what happens
in the cab to the hotel.

What with light might we imagine? When
a storm blows in at night and clouds explode
the sky, this monster city turns ancient village
and shudders until morning. A little girl stomps
through alley puddles chasing pigeons. She
doesn't tire; she never will. A square-headed
boy joins her, more interested in feeding
than stomping. Each new day shadows slant
across stone into night, then it's dawn
again for a thousand years. Is there more miracle
than children growing into men and women?
Don't forget the righteous rage and white light
of bombs every night somewhere in the world
even as, especially as you watch morning
find its way past the brick dome over your bed
to bathe her skin in yellow. And in the newest
darkness, as far as you know the last you'll ever
see, names gone, remember the lay of light
through bars onto baskets of purple garlic.

Also by **David Allan Cates**

Novels

HUNGER IN AMERICA
X OUT OF WONDERLAND
FREEMAN WALKER
BEN ARMSTRONG'S STRANGE TRIP HOME
TOM CONNOR'S GIFT

Short Story Collections

IMAGINING TANYA

Poetry Chapbooks

THE MYSTERIOUS LOCATION OF KYRGYZSTAN

David **Allan Cates** is the author of five award-winning novels, a collection of short stories, and a chapbook of poetry. He's published dozens of short stories and poems in literary magazines, and his essays and travel articles have appeared in Outside Magazine and the New York Times Sophisticated Traveler. He was born in Wisconsin, raised cattle on his family's farm, worked on construction sites, in offices, restaurants, and on boats. He's driven a taxi, played professional basketball in Costa Rica, and was a medical interpreter in rural clinics and hospitals in Honduras. He has taught writing at all levels, from prison classes, to public high schools, to universities, to hospitals. He currently teaches private students, and serves as the director of Missoula Medical Aid, an NGO that provides public health and surgical services in Honduras, and supports nutrition and agricultural development projects there. He and his wife raised three daughters, and live in Montana.